LEWIS & CLARK

THE JOURNEY HOME

JOHN HAMILTON

Published by ABDO & Daughters, an imprint of ABDO Publishing Company, 4940 Viking Drive, Suite 622, Edina, Minnesota 55435. Copyright ©2003 by Abdo Consulting Group, Inc. International copyrights reserved in all countries. No part of this book may be reproduced in any form without written permission from the publisher.

Printed in the United States.

Edited by Paul Joseph
Graphic Design: John Hamilton
Cover Design: Mighty Media
Photos and illustrations:
  John Hamilton, Cover, p. 1, 4-5, 8, 9, 14-15, 16, 19, 24, 29
  American Philosophical Society, p. 10, 11
  Beinecke Museum, Karl Bodmer, p. 22
  Getty Museum, William Henry Jackson, p. 25
  Image Club Graphics, Karl Bodmer, p. 23; Olaf Carl Seltzer, p. 26
  John F. Clymer, Clymer Museum of Art, p. 18, 20
  Joslyn Art Museum, Karl Bodmer, p. 27
  Library of Congress, W. Clark, p. 3, 28, 30-31; E.S. Curtis, p. 7, 13, 21
  National Museum of American Art, Charles Bird King, p. 6

Library of Congress Cataloging-in-Publication Data

Hamilton, John, 1959-
    The journey home / John Hamilton.
    p. cm.—(Lewis & Clark)
    Includes index.
    Summary: Joins the Lewis and Clark Expedition in the spring of 1806 as its members leave Fort Clatsop and return home, then continue their separate lives. Includes highlights and directions to historical points of interest.
    ISBN 1-57765-766-7
    1. Lewis and Clark Expedition (1804-1806)—Juvenile literature. 2. West (U.S.)—Discovery and exploration—Juvenile literature. 3. West (U.S.)—Description and travel—Juvenile literature.
[1. Lewis and Clark Expedition (1804-1806) 2. West (U.S.)—Discovery and exploration.]
    I. Title.

F592.7.H26 2002
917.804'2—dc21

2001053400

TABLE OF CONTENTS

"we loaded our Canoes & at 1 P.M. left Fort Clatsop on our homeward bound journey. At this place we had wintered and remained from the 7th of Decr. 1805 to this day and have lived as well as we had any right to expect."

WILLIAM CLARK, MARCH 23, 1806

HOMEWARD BOUND

In January 1806, a group of 45 Native Americans from 11 different tribes visited President Thomas Jefferson in Washington, D.C. The president welcomed the delegation of Missouri, Oto, Arikara, and Yankton Sioux chiefs, and arranged for a tour of the city so they could witness the power of the United States. They talked about trade and how the Indians could benefit from American companies setting up outposts in Louisiana Territory. Jefferson stressed how important it was that the tribes be at peace with one another so that the United States and the Native American tribes could "all live together as one household."

The chiefs were impressed with U.S. technology and the country's huge cities. They also spoke highly of Lewis and Clark, who had visited the tribes on their way west the previous year. It was through Lewis and Clark's invitation that the Indians were visiting Washington, D.C. President Jefferson referred to Lewis as "our beloved man," and thanked the Native American chiefs for the kindness they had shown the Corps of Discovery.

Charles Bird King painted this portrait of Omaha, Kansas, Missouri, and Pawnee Indians during their visit to the east in 1821. The man in front is wearing a Jefferson peace medal.

The chiefs responded, "We have seen the beloved man, we shook hands with him and we heard the words you put in his mouth. We wish him well… We have him in our hearts, and when he will return we believe that he will take care of us, prevent our wants and make us happy."

Despite their friendship with Lewis and Clark, the chiefs were troubled. White settlers were starting to take over Native American lands. The delegation gave this warning to Jefferson: "When you tell us that your children of this side of the Mississippi hear your word, you are mistaken, since every day they raise their tomahawks over our heads… Tell your white children on our lands to follow your orders and to do not as they please, for they do not keep your word."

President Jefferson assured the chiefs that he would do all he could to make sure settlers obeyed treaties with the Native Americans. But in reality, there wasn't much Jefferson could do. On the vast, lawless frontier, trappers and prospectors were starting what would become a tidal wave of settlements, and there was no way to stop them. It was the beginning of the end for the Indian nations.

Jefferson wrote a note to Lewis's mother and brother. He told them he was confident that Lewis was alive and well. But privately, in a letter to naturalist William Dunbar, Jefferson wrote, "We have no certain information of Capt. Lewis since he left Fort Mandan." A year had passed since the Corps had left the Mandan villages in present-day North Dakota. Nobody knew for sure what had become of the explorers. All Jefferson could do was wait and hope.

"Not any occurences today worthy of notice."

WILLIAM CLARK

As President Jefferson met with the Native American chiefs, Meriwether Lewis, William Clark, and the Corps of Discovery were stuck in Fort Clatsop, enduring a typical stormy, damp Oregon winter. The fort was a cramped, wooden stockade. It was near a river a few miles upstream from where the Columbia River empties into the Pacific Ocean. The men's spirits were sapped by the dampness brought on by almost continual bad weather. During their stay, there were only 12 days without rain, and only six with sunshine.

Everybody was homesick. Routine at the camp was unbearably dull. The food was bad, and everything was soggy. Most of the men suffered from colds or flu. The local Clatsop and Chinook Indians were doing well, but they demanded payment for food and trade goods. The Corps was nearly out of the presents it used as money to pay the Indians, and it still had half a continent to cross. The only thing the expedition had plenty of were rifles and lead, and pens and ink for the journals.

After five long months on the Pacific coast, they hadn't spotted a single ship. They had hoped to hitch a ride home, or at least send copies of their precious journals back to President Jefferson by sea, but it was not to be.

The men had pent-up energy and were ready to go home. On March 23, 1806, they set their canoes in the water and began the long journey home. Before they left, they stole a badly needed canoe from the Clatsop Indians.

Throughout the trip Lewis and Clark had been respectful of the Native Americans they met. The Indians remembered Lewis and Clark for their honesty and friendliness. Yet Lewis ordered his men to steal a canoe. He badly needed another boat, but couldn't afford the high prices the Clatsops were charging. In his journal, Lewis justified the theft by saying it was in exchange for six elk the Clatsops stole from the Corps. He didn't mention, however, that the Indians later paid for the elk.

Without the Clatsops' help, the Corps might not have survived that winter. The stolen canoe was a friendship betrayed, a lapse of judgement that tarnished the Corps's reputation.

Edward S. Curtis took this photograph of a canoe built by Indians of the Pacific Northwest.

"Even now I shudder with the expectation of great dificuelties in passing those Mountains, from the debth of snow and the want of grass sufficient for [our] horses."

WILLIAM CLARK

Back to the Mountains

Paddling upstream against the current of the Columbia River was hard work, and the going was slow. The spring salmon run had not yet begun, and food was scarce. Indians along the riverbanks that the Corps met charged high prices for food.

The expedition had to portage its heavy canoes over the many falls and rapids of the Columbia. As they hauled their gear along the shore, Indians constantly followed the men, harassing them and stealing small items such as axes or tomahawks.

One day a group of Indians even stole Lewis's big Newfoundland dog, Seaman. Lewis was so enraged he ordered his men to march into a native village and burn it down unless his dog was returned. Luckily for all involved, the thieves gave back the dog after a brief chase.

A pair of elk graze in a mountain meadow. After months of living on nothing but elk, roots, and fish, the men of the Corps were anxious to get back to the Great Plains, where buffalo were plentiful.

"April 11th. Many of the natives crouded about the bank of the river where the men were engaged in taking up the canoes; one of them had the insolence to cast stones down... at the men... These are the greatest thieves and scoundrels we have met with..."

MERIWETHER LEWIS

Lewis drew this small eulachon, also called a candlefish, in his journal while at Fort Clatsop. He wrote, "I think them superior to any fish I ever tasted."

Lewis had developed a very short temper. Once, when a saddle and robe were stolen, he again threatened to burn down a village. Violence was averted when the items were eventually found. Some historians think Lewis was suffering from depression, which ran in his family. Or it could be that he was worried for the safety of his men. They had endured so much, traveled so far, and discovered so many things. But it would all be for nothing if they couldn't get themselves, the journals, and the scientific specimens back to civilization.

There were many obstacles yet to come, not the least of which were the Bitterroots, the same terrible mountains that had nearly killed them the previous autumn. In his journal, Lewis tried to steady his nerves by reminding himself, "Patience, patience."

At Celilo Falls, the expedition abandoned the river. They bought 13 ponies at very high prices from a local Indian tribe. Traveling overland was faster than paddling against the swift river current, but the journey was still difficult. They didn't have much success hunting for food. Instead, they bought dogs to eat from the Indians, just as they had done on the westward journey. To help pay for the dogs, Clark exchanged medical services, which the Indians gladly accepted.

When the Corps reached the territory of the Walla Walla tribe, their chief, Yellept, greeted the expedition warmly. They stayed three days, relaxing and exchanging gifts. Their relationship was much friendlier than with the Indians they encountered on the lower part of the Columbia. Of the Walla Wallas, Lewis wrote, "I think we can justly affirm to the honor of these people that they are the most hospitable, honest, and sincere people that we have met with in our voyage."

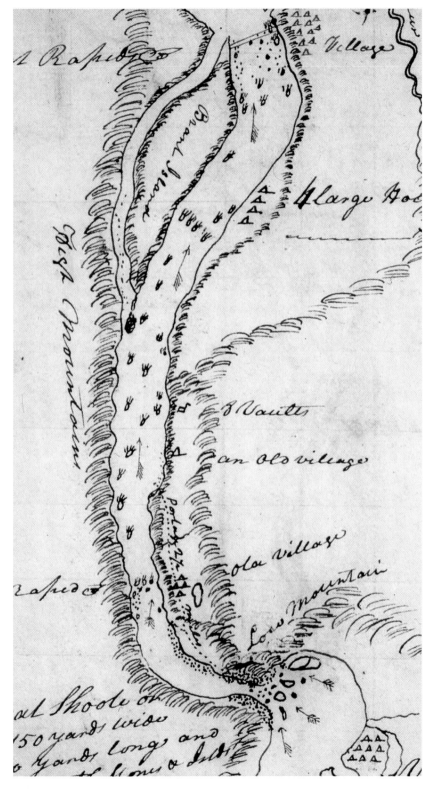

This map by William Clark shows a series of rapids on the Columbia River. When going upstream, the Corps had to portage its canoes around the swift water.

By early May, the Corps was back in Nez Percé land, where they also received a warm welcome. They met their old friend and guide Chief Twisted Hair, and rounded up most of the horses the tribe had kept for them over the winter. They were forced to stay with the Nez Percé for several weeks. Snow was still too deep on the Lolo Trail, which spanned the Bitterroot Mountains.

"May 7th. This is unwelcom inteligence to men confined to a diet of horsebeef and roots, and who are as anxious as we are to return to the fat plains of the Missouri and thence to our native homes."

MERIWETHER LEWIS

As they waited for the mountain snows to recede, they spent the next four weeks keeping in shape by playing athletic games with the young Nez Percé warriors. They competed in foot races and shooting matches. The Indians were impressed, especially by Captain Lewis's marksmanship. They also played a new game called base, an early version of baseball.

On horseback, it was the Nez Percé who put the Americans to shame. The Indians rode at breakneck speed, and could shoot arrows at a moving target with pinpoint accuracy, even at a full gallop.

One of the Nez Percé chiefs gave Lewis and Clark horses, and refused to take any payment. At a tribal council, the Nez Percé made a promise that they would always be at peace with Lewis and Clark, and the United States.

On June 10, after four weeks with the Nez Percé, the expedition packed up and set off across Weippe Prairie, heading for the Bitterroots. Chief Twisted Hair told them it was still too snowy up in the mountains, but Lewis and Clark couldn't wait any longer. All the men looked forward to crossing the mountains and descending onto the Great Plains, where herds of buffalo awaited.

"Here was winter with all it's rigors… The air was cold, my hands and feet were benumbed."

MERIWETHER LEWIS

They soon discovered they had been too hasty. In less than a week they found themselves in snow 12 feet (3.7 m) deep, and couldn't find the trail. For the first time in the entire expedition, they were forced to retreat.

On June 24, they tried again, this time with several Nez Percé, most of them teenage boys. The captains wrote several times of how impressed they were of the woodsman skills of their guides. Food was scarce and the temperatures were freezing, but it was easier going than when they had crossed the year before, thanks in large part to their guides.

By the end of June, they descended to the camp they called Traveler's Rest, at the end of the Lolo Trail. The ordeal of the mountains was finally behind them.

Edward S. Curtis took this picture of a member of the Nez Percé tribe a century after Lewis and Clark passed through tribal lands.

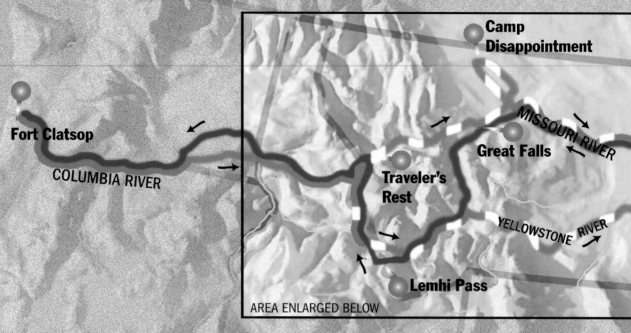

Camp
Disappointment

Fort Clatsop

COLUMBIA RIVER

Traveler's
Rest

MISSOURI RIVER

Great Falls

YELLOWSTONE RIVER

Lemhi Pass

AREA ENLARGED BELOW

Camp Disappointment

Blackfeet

MARIAS RIVER

MISSOURI RIVER

Lewis's return, 1806

Great Falls

Nez
Percé

Lolo Trail

Traveler's
Rest

CLEARWATER RIVER

Three Forks

YELLOWSTONE RIVER

JEFFERSON RIVER

Clark's return, 1806

Shoshone

Lemhi Pass

Fort Mandan

Teton Sioux

MISSOURI RIVER

Yankton
Sioux

Floyd's
Grave

Camp
Dubois

St. Louis

Meriwether Lewis

William Clark

LEGEND

Westbound route, 1804-1805

Return route, 1806

Lewis & Clark separate routes

Lewis
&
Clark

"July 13th. The indian woman, who has been of great service to me as a pilot through this country, recommends a gap in the mountain more south, which I shall cross."
WILLIAM CLARK

DOWN THE YELLOWSTONE

*A*t Traveler's Rest, Lewis and Clark announced a complicated and daring plan. They would split up the expedition so they could explore more of the Louisiana Territory. Lewis knew that President Jefferson would be disappointed that there was no Northwest Passage, no easy water route across the continent. Lewis hoped they could find a better path than the one they took the previous year, when they had traveled westward.

It was a bold scheme, and probably unwise. They would split into small groups and would be hundreds of miles from each other. While Lewis and several volunteers explored a shortcut to the Great Falls of the Missouri, and then searched for the source of the Marias River, most of the men would return to the Three Forks area of the Missouri River. Once at the Three Forks, they would split up again. Some would float down the river to the Great Falls, where they would dig up the canoes and supplies they had buried the previous year. Clark would take a small group overland until they hit the Yellowstone River, then rejoin the main expedition where the river emptied into the Missouri.

It was a plan full of danger, but Lewis and Clark now had enough confidence in their men to risk it. They promised to reunite in one month, then said their good-byes.

"July 3rd. I took leave of my worthy friend and companion, Capt. Clark, and the party that accompanyed him. I could not avoid feeling much concern on this occasion although I hoped this seperation was only momentary."

MERIWETHER LEWIS

Far left: The Yellowstone River winds past a network of sandstone cliffs near present-day Billings, Montana

Artist John Clymer's *A Gangue of Buffalow* shows Clark's group being stopped on the Yellowstone River by a giant herd of bison crossing the water

When Clark's group reached the Three Forks, Sergeant John Ordway and nine men set off downstream in canoes they had buried at the Beaverhead River the previous autumn. All the supplies they had cached were damp but safe.

Clark headed east, traveling overland on horseback. He took with him a small group, including his slave York, Toussaint Charbonneau, Sacagawea, and her baby, Jean Baptiste.

Sacagawea knew the countryside. She had taken trips in the area when she was a young girl. For the first time on the expedition, she acted as an actual guide, showing them a shortcut across today's Bozeman Pass in Montana.

Clark's group reached the Yellowstone River on July 15. They hollowed out two big cottonwood trees to make canoes. In the middle of the night, Indians stole many of their horses.

The group lashed the two canoes together to make a raft, then floated down the Yellowstone. Soon they were on the Great Plains again, with plentiful game to hunt. The men were especially eager to hunt buffalo, which they craved after surviving on a diet of roots, dogmeat, and horsemeat.

Insect pests were another familiar sight on the plains. As they floated down one section of the river, Clark wrote that grasshoppers "had destroyed every sprig of grass for miles." Mosquitoes tormented them. "The Mosquetoes," Clark wrote, "are more troublesome than ever we have seen them before."

The animal herds they saw were immense. Once they had to stop the canoes and wait an hour for an immense herd of buffalo to swim across the river ahead of them.

On July 25, Clark discovered a big sandstone outcropping on the south bank of the river, near what is now Billings, Montana. He called it Pompy's Tower, after Sacagawea's son, Jean Baptiste. Clark had grown fond of the little boy, and nicknamed him Little Pomp.

Clark climbed up the side of the rock and etched his name and the date into the soft sandstone. It is the only physical evidence of the Corps of Discovery that can still be seen today.

Above, top: Pompy's Tower, called Pompey's Pillar today
Above: Clark's inscription

John Clymer's *The Lewis Crossing* shows Lewis and his group crossing the Clark Fork River, near present-day Missoula, Montana. Nez Percé guides helped Lewis part of the way.

THE MARIAS EXPLORATION

A s Clark drifted down the Yellowstone River, Lewis was hundreds of miles away to the northwest. After dropping off some of his men at the Great Falls of Montana, his small group set out to explore the Marias River. The terms of the Louisiana Purchase said that the land included the drainage of the Missouri River and all its tributaries. Lewis hoped that the Marias ran far to the north, into Canada. If so, it would give the United States claim to land that England wanted.

Accompanying Lewis were George Drouillard and the two Field brothers, Joseph and Reuben. After several days, they camped near the northernmost reach of the Marias, close to the eastern edge of present-day Glacier National Park.

To Lewis's dismay, the river didn't stretch into Canada. He called the area Camp Disappointment. After two days of rest, he and his small group headed back toward the Missouri River.

They were now deep into Blackfeet Indian country, and Lewis was nervous. Other tribes the Corps had encountered all feared the Blackfeet. They controlled trade on the northern plains, and they had connections with the British, which meant they were well supplied with rifles and horses. Even though Lewis was supposed to set up peaceful trade relations with Native Americans, he hoped to avoid meeting the Blackfeet. He didn't have enough men to defend against an attack if the Blackfeet proved hostile.

On July 26, Lewis looked through his telescope and spied eight Blackfeet warriors watching the Americans. "This was a very unpleasant sight," he later wrote.

Despite his fears, Lewis met with the Indians, giving them gifts of handkerchiefs and peace medals to ease the tension. With nightfall approaching, they all camped under the shade of three small cottonwood trees.

Photographer Edward S. Curtis's *In Blackfoot Country*

Artist Karl Bodmer painted this Blackfeet portrait in the 1830s

Lewis told the Indians that the Americans had set up trade with the Shoshones and Nez Percé, and that they wanted trade relations with the Blackfeet also. But the warriors weren't happy. With American trade goods, especially weapons, being handed to their enemies, the Blackfeet monopoly on trade was threatened, their power diminished. Lewis was bringing the worst possible news to the Blackfeet.

At the first light of morning, Lewis was startled awake by shouting. He saw Joseph Field fighting with one of the Blackfeet, who had tried to steal Field's rifle. Reuben Field, while trying to take back his own rifle, had already stabbed one of the Blackfeet to death.

"I then drew a pistol from my holster and terning myself about saw the indian making off with my gun. I ran at him with my pistol and bid him lay down my gun, which he was in the act of doing when the Fieldes returned and drew up their guns to shoot him, which I forbade as he did not appear to be about to make any resistance or commit any offensive act... He droped the gun and walked slowly off."

MERIWETHER LEWIS

Lewis recovered his rifle, but two other Blackfeet were rounding up the men's horses. Lewis ran to stop them. One hid behind a rock. As Lewis ran forward, the other warrior wheeled about, rifle in hand.

"At a distance of 30 steps... I shot him through the belly. He fell to his knees and on his wright elbow, from which position he partly raised himself up and fired at me, and turning himself about crawled in behind a rock... He overshot me, [but] being bearheaded I felt the wind of his bullet very distinctly."

MERIWETHER LEWIS

Lewis and his men got their weapons back, but two Blackfeet were dead. The other six warriors had fled, running off toward their main camp. Lewis was sure a war party would soon be chasing them, looking for revenge. He and his men immediately rounded up their horses and set off in a rush across the prairie.

They ran their horses for 24 hours, continuing even in the dark of night. After fleeing for 120 miles (193 km), they finally made it back to the Missouri River.

As if by a miracle, at that moment they met the combined expedition groups from the Great Falls, rounding a bend in the river. Lewis and his men abandoned their horses and leaped into the canoes. Then they were off, racing downriver to safety.

Frontier artist Karl Bodmer painted this portrait of a Piegan warrior. The Piegans were members of the Blackfeet tribe.

"September 17th. [Another] Gentleman informed us that we had been long Since given up by the people of the U.S.... and almost forgotton. [But] the President of the U. States had yet hopes of us."

WILLIAM CLARK

JOURNEY'S END

On August 12, the two groups of explorers linked up near the intersection of the Missouri and Yellowstone Rivers. The two captains traded stories of their adventures and narrow escapes. The only major injury had happened to Lewis a few days earlier. While out hunting, Pierre Cruzatte mistook Lewis for an elk and shot him in the buttocks. The bullet entered one buttock and passed through the other. It was a painful wound, but Lewis was walking again in three weeks. During his recovery he had to lie flat on his belly in a canoe.

The Corps sailed down the swift-flowing current of the Missouri, sometimes covering more than 80 miles (129 km) a day. Two days after meeting at the Yellowstone, they stopped at the Mandan villages to visit their old friends. They gave Charbonneau his pay, and said good-bye to Sacagawea and her son. Clark had grown fond of Jean Baptiste, a "butifull promising child." He offered to raise and educate him back east. Clark later wrote, "They observed that in one year the boy would be sufficiently old to leave his mother… if I would be so friendly as to raise the child in such a manner as I thought proper, to which I agreed."

The men of the Corps also said good-bye to one of their own, John Colter. He had fallen in love with the wild frontier, and asked to join two trappers who were planning to go up the Yellowstone to hunt for beaver. The captains granted Colter an early discharge. He later became one of the first mountain men, and the first white man to see what is today Yellowstone National Park.

An 1870 photo of Yellowstone National Park's Old Faithful geyser, by William Henry Jackson

Olaf Carl Seltzer's *Prowlers of the Prairie*

After a three-day stay with the Mandans, the Corps proceeded on once more. They practically flew down the river, eager to be home. As they passed the lands of the Teton Sioux, the tribe that had given them so much trouble in the autumn of 1804, they saw Chief Black Buffalo hailing them from a hilltop. The Corps refused to stop. Clark shouted to the chief, telling him they remembered how poorly they had been treated, and that the Teton Sioux were "bad people." In response, Black Buffalo cursed the Corps by striking his rifle three times on the ground.

Near present-day Sioux City, Iowa, they stopped to pay their respects to Sergeant Charles Floyd. He was the only man killed on the expedition, which many consider a miracle, considering all the hardships they endured.

As they sped home with the current, they started to encounter boats coming upriver, traders and fur trappers hoping to profit in the new territories. The Lewis and Clark expedition had opened a floodgate of exploration and settlement. The men eagerly listened to news of the past two and a half years. They learned that most people back home had given them up for dead.

On September 20, the men saw a cow grazing near shore. They raised a cheer: it was the first sign that they were approaching civilization. When they reached the tiny outpost of La Charette, the citizens were "much astonished in seeing us return."

On September 23, 1806, the men of the Corps of Discovery spent their last day together. They arrived at the mouth of the Missouri River, then drifted downstream on the Mississippi, stopping briefly at Camp Dubois, where they had spent the winter of 1803-1804.

Karl Bodmer painted this scene of Missouri River traders and their keelboat. As Lewis and Clark came down the Missouri in 1806, they met many boats filled with traders and fur trappers heading into Louisiana Territory.

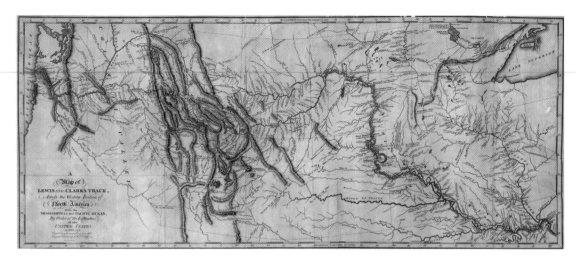

This is William Clark's map of North America, which many consider a masterpiece of cartography. To draw the map, he combined compass readings, distances, and sketches he drew while on the journey. He also used information from Indians, traders, and other explorers.

At noon they came within sight of St. Louis. After 8,000 miles (12,875 km) and 28 months, Lewis and Clark had returned. The entire town gathered to watch and celebrate.

"Fired three rounds as we approached… and landed oppocit the center of the Town. The people gathred on the Shore and Huzzared three cheers… then the party considerable much rejoiced that we have the Expedition Completed.

"And now we look for boarding in Town and wait for our settlement, and then we entend to return to our native homes to See our parents once more, as we have been So long from them."

JOHN ORDWAY

The country treated them like national heroes. It was as if they had returned from the moon. Lewis made his report to a grateful President Jefferson. As a reward, Congress gave the men double pay, plus 320 acres (129 hectares) of land. The captains each received 1,600 acres (647 hectares).

Lewis and Clark and the Corps of Discovery were trailblazers, the first United States citizens to cross the continent. They were the first to explore uncharted territory west of the Mississippi. They mapped the land, described 178 plants and 122 animals new to science, and met with dozens of Native American tribes. It was their great journey that opened the West to American expansion. This band of heroes uncovered a land rich with possibilities. Two hundred years later, we still follow in their footsteps.

"The work we are now doing is, I trust, done for posterity, in such a way that they need not repeat it... We shall delineate with correctness the great arteries of this great country; those who come after us will... fill up the canvas we begin."

THOMAS JEFFERSON

THEY PROCEEDED ON

MERIWETHER LEWIS (1774-1809)

After co-commanding the Corps of Discovery, Lewis became governor of Louisiana Territory while living in St. Louis. It wasn't a job he was suited for. He was also unlucky in love. He courted several women, but was turned down each time. Lewis drank heavily. He also suffered from depression, made worse by an addiction to opium, which he took to fight malaria. In 1809, Lewis traveled to Washington, D.C., to straighten out financial problems. Along the way, he became more and more distraught over his troubles. On a trail called the Natchez Trace in Tennessee, Meriwether Lewis took his own life.

WILLIAM CLARK (1770-1838)

Clark served as governor of Missouri Territory from 1813 to 1820. He lived in St. Louis with his wife, Julia, whom he had named a river after. From 1813 until his death at age 69, he was in charge of Indian affairs west of the Mississippi River. Native Americans, most of whom considered him their good friend, called Clark "the Red-Headed Chief." He died in the home of his eldest son, Meriwether Lewis Clark.

SACAGAWEA (1788?-1812?)

Not much is known about Sacagawea's life after the expedition. She continued living with her husband, Toussaint Charbonneau, at the Knife River Indian villages. In 1809, they traveled to St. Louis with their son, Jean Baptiste. William Clark became the boy's guardian. In 1812, at Fort Manuel in present-day South Dakota, she gave birth to a baby girl, Lisette. That winter, Sacagawea became ill and died.

YORK (1770?-1832?)

In 1811, several years after the expedition, William Clark finally granted York his freedom. York started a freighting business in Tennessee and Kentucky. He died probably of cholera sometime around 1832.

GEORGE DROUILLARD (?-1810)

George Drouillard, the expedition's best hunter, joined a fur company started by Manuel Lisa. In 1810, he helped establish Lisa's trading post at Three Forks. While there, Drouillard was killed in a fight with Blackfeet Indians.

GLOSSARY

CACHE

A place where explorers hide food and supplies. Lewis and Clark cached supplies and canoes in several places, including the Beaverhead River and at the Great Falls of Montana. Knowing that they would return along the same route, they buried items they couldn't use the rest of the way westward, such as the large oversized canoes called pirgoues. They also cached many of the scientific specimens they collected. On at least one occasion river water seeped into a cache, ruining many of the specimens and notes.

CORPS

A branch of the military that has a specialized function.

GREAT PLAINS

A huge, sloping region of valleys and plains in west-central North America. The Great Plains extend from Texas to southern Canada, and from the Rocky Mountains nearly 400 miles (644 km) to the east.

PORTAGE

To carry a boat and supplies overland from one lake or river to another. The Corps of Discovery portaged around the Great Falls of Montana for more than 18 miles (29 km).

WEB SITES

Would you like to learn more about Lewis & Clark? Please visit **www.abdopub.com** to find up-to-date Web site links about Lewis & Clark and the Corps of Discovery. These links are routinely monitored and updated to provide the most current information available.

INDEX